PENNY & MARIA
THE DONKEY'S JOURNEY TO THE TEMPLE OF ATHENA

A Dream Come True

PAULA ANDRES

AuthorHouse™
1663 Liberty Drive
Bloomington, IN 47403
www.authorhouse.com
Phone: 833-262-8899

Because of the dynamic nature of the Internet, any web addresses or links contained in this
book may have changed since publication and may no longer be valid. The views expressed
in this work are solely those of the author and do not necessarily reflect the views of
the publisher, and the publisher hereby disclaims any responsibility for them.

Any people depicted in stock imagery provided by Getty Images are models,
and such images are being used for illustrative purposes only.
Certain stock imagery © Getty Images.

This book is printed on acid-free paper.

ISBN: 978-1-6655-6268-3 (sc)
ISBN: 978-1-6655-6269-0 (e)

Library of Congress Control Number: 2022911301

Print information available on the last page.

Published by AuthorHouse 06/15/2022

authorHOUSE®

PENNY & MARIA

THE DONKEY'S JOURNEY TO THE TEMPLE OF ATHENA

Penny and her family traveled to the Greek Island of Rhodes to see the Temple of Athena. It was on top of a mountain in the village of Lindos. They could either walk up the steep marble steps to the top or take a donkey ride. Of course, Penny begged to ride the donkey. It was something she always dreamed of doing. The family was going to walk to the temple, but when her parents saw that the other children on the tour were riding the donkeys, they agreed to let Penny do the same.

"I'm so excited", Penny shouted as she ran to join the other children. "My wish is finally going to come true."

The donkey's owner, Kosta, was going to lead them up to the temple on the donkeys. He had eight of them lined up on the narrow cobblestone street that curved through the village and out into an open field on the edge of the mountain.

Penny looked around and realized she was the last one in line to get a donkey. She turned to count how many others were ahead of her.

"I can't believe it!" Penny cried. "I am number 9 in line, and there are only 8 donkeys! That means I can't go on the ride!"

Her eyes started to fill with tears as she looked down at the ground and stomped her foot. "Now I'll have to go with my parents and walk to the top of the mountain on those slippery marble steps."

Penny had started to walk away from the line, but as she looked up, she saw Kosta coming from the barn with one more donkey!

"Hooray, I do get to go on the donkey ride!" she cheered.

Penny grinned from ear to ear and ran back to the end of the line.

She watched excitedly as Kosta and the donkey walked toward her. But something didn't look right.

The donkey kept trying to walk backwards toward the barn, pulling against the owner. Penny had heard that donkeys could be stubborn, so she guessed everything was okay after all.

When Kosta and the donkey finally reached Penny, he introduced the donkey as Maria.

"You have the prettiest big eyes, and you are just the right size for me. I'm so excited to be able to ride you!" Penny exclaimed.

Penny patted the top of Maria's head. The mane on top of her head and down her neck was short. It felt sort of picky like Penny's hairbrush, but the fur around it was soft and very warm. Maria's long ears stood tall on top of her head and felt like velvet.

Maria heard Penny say how excited she was to finally ride her, so the tired donkey would now have to go to the ruins of the Temple of Athena. Maria thought to herself, "If Penny knew how many people sat on me this week, she would know that her excitement doesn't help. I just want to rest!

I'm always the one who leads the group when the tourists come through. Kosta saw my sore leg this morning, and he was going to let me stay in the barn. Today is supposed to be my day to rest. But then, this one last girl shows up. Kosta would never disappoint a child, so I'll have to go to the top of the mountain again today."

"I just know this is going to be a very special ride!" Penny exclaimed.

Penny loved her new friend and was even more excited when the owner led Maria to the front of the line to lead the others.

Kosta walked back and forth along the line of donkeys as they slowly strolled on the cobblestone streets between the stucco walls of the village.

"Something is wrong with Maria. She keeps trying to push me against the wall!" yelled Penny.

Maria was heading into the stucco wall, scraping Penny's leg against the tiny, sharp white points of the stucco. Penny tried to pull the donkey away from the wall, but Maria kept drifting back.

"Maria, stop that!" Penny cried. "Why are you trying to hurt me? My leg is getting all scratched up!"

Penny tried to lift her leg onto the saddle, so she wouldn't get hurt, but she couldn't get it out from between Maria and the wall.

Maria groaned inside, "I'm so tired and my leg is really sore. I don't want to go to the top of that mountain again!"

Maria sensed Penny's fears and heard her yelling, but Maria didn't care. She was exhausted from these daily walks and was in pain. The tired, sore donkey just wanted to be in the barn.

Kosta ran to the front of the line when he heard Penny screaming. He stopped the group for a moment to check her leg.

"Penny, it's okay", Kosta explained. "We are leaving the village now and going out into the open field. Your leg is okay, just a little red."

As Kosta led the group on the curved path past the village walls and into the open field, Penny took a deep breath and relaxed as she saw the beautiful view of the mountains and hills in the distance.

The path from the village opened to a beautiful, but rocky field with a narrow dirt path that ran along the edge of the cliff. The sun was warm, and the sky was deep blue, just like the Mediterranean Sea that you could see and smell in the distance. Looking ahead, Penny could see the Temple of Athena, sitting on top of the mountain with its white marble columns shining in the sunlight.

She also saw the people walking up those steep steps all the way to the top.

"This donkey is trying to push me over the side of the cliff," Penny screamed. "She hates me!

Why is she so close to the edge of the mountain? First she tried to squash me against the walls in the village, and now she's trying to throw me over the mountainside!"

Penny looked down and all she could see was the jagged edge of the cliff next to the path. She was so high up; she couldn't see what was at the bottom of the mountain. It seemed the farther they walked, the closer Maria got to the edge! Penny could hardly see any path left between her and the rocky ledge.

Maria grumbled to herself, "On top of having a sore leg and being tired, now I have a sore neck from being pulled so hard by Penny.

Why does this girl keep tugging and pulling my reins to the side, and why won't she stop screaming at me? She is hurting my neck. Every time I try to pull back, she pulls harder the other way. I know where I am going!

Doesn't Penny understand that I'm not trying to do anything to hurt her? My leg is so sore. That's why I kept leaning to one side when we started walking through the village. Now I'm just trying to take the path I've been trained to walk. I'm not trying to purposely hurt anyone. I'm just uncomfortable and hurting.

And now, besides hurting me, she is yelling at Kosta. I've never heard him so upset!"

Kosta ran toward Penny, yelled at her to stop, and took the reins away from her.

"Stop that! Stop pulling on those reins and stop screaming. You're upsetting the other children behind you!

Maria knows exactly where she is going. She walks this path almost every day.

Donkeys are very sure-footed and keep their balance well. I am sorry you are so frightened. You need to understand that trained animals do what they are taught. They don't think about things like trying to hurt people."

Once Penny heard what Kosta told her, she felt better.

"Look, Penny, there are your parents over there by the steps," Kosta continued. "I will keep the reins and lead Maria over to them."

Penny was very happy to see her parents.

Kosta helped her get down off of Maria.

Once she got down, Penny turned and gave Maria a big hug around her solid, warm, soft neck.

"I'm sorry I yelled and pulled at you, Maria." Penny exclaimed. "You really are a good little donkey!"

Maria thought to herself, "Penny kept telling Kosta that I was causing all her problems. Actually, she was causing more commotion than I ever could. I'm just doing what I was taught to do.

I wish humans would stop thinking that we act and think like they do."

Maria watched Penny running happily to her parents.

Now it was time for Maria to return to the barn and rest.

Even with all the day's excitement, Maria the donkey was glad Penny's dream came true, and she could be a part of her very special day.

Printed in the United States
by Baker & Taylor Publisher Services